Halloween Spirits and Other Tales:

The Coming of Harvest

Halloween Spirits and Other Tales:

The Coming of Harvest

By

SIMON KING

CONSCIOUS CARE PUBLISHING PTY LTD

Halloween Spirits and Other Tales
The Coming of Harvest

Copyright © 2020 by Simon King. All rights reserved.

First Published 2020 by: Conscious Care Publishing Pty Ltd
PO Box 776, Rockingham, WA 6968, Australia
www.consciouscarepublishing.com

First Edition printed May 2020.

Notice of Rights
This book is sold subject to the condition that it shall not, by way of trade or otherwise, be lent, resold, hired out, or otherwise circulated without the publisher's prior consent, in any form of binding or cover, other than that in which it is published, and without a similar condition, including this condition being imposed on the subsequent purchaser. All rights reserved by the publisher. No part of this publication may be reproduced, stored in a retrieval system, or transmitted in any form, or by any means, electronic, digital, mechanical, photocopying, scanning, recorded or otherwise, without the prior written permission of the copyright owner. Requests to the copyright owner should be addressed to Permissions Department, Conscious Care Publishing Pty Ltd, PO Box 776, Rockingham, WA 6968, Australia, email: admin@conscious-carepublishing.com

Limits of Liability/Disclaimer of Warranty:
While the publisher and author have used their best efforts in preparing this book, they make no representations or warranties with respect to the accuracy or completeness of the contents of this book and specifically disclaim any implied warranties of merchantability or fitness for a particular purpose. No warranty may be created or extended by sales representatives or written sales materials. The advice and strategies contained herein may not be suitable for your situation. You should consult with a professional where appropriate. The intent of the author is only to offer information for a general nature. Neither the publisher nor author shall be liable for any loss of profit or any other commercial damages, including but not limited to special, incidental, consequential, or other damages. The author and the publisher assume no responsibility for your actions.

Where photographic images have been provided by the author and people are depicted, such images are being used for illustrative purposes only. Product names may be trademarks or registered trademarks, and are used for identification and explanation without intent to infringe. Conscious Care Publishing publishes in a variety of print and electronic format and by print-on-demand. Some material included with standard print versions of this book may not be included in e-books or in print-on-demand. If this book refers to media such as a CD or DVD that is not included in the version you purchased, you may download this material at www.conscious-carepublishing.com

National Library of Australia Cataloguing-in-Publication entry:
Author: King, Simon 1950-
Extraterrestrial / by Simon King
ISBN 9780987633774 (Paperback)
Rocky Hudson, Editor.

Printed by Lightning Source
Typeset & cover design by Conscious Care Publishing Pty Ltd

ISBN: 978-0-9876337-7-4

DEDICATION

This book is dedicated to those among us who actively participate in the spirit of Hallowe'en and all the revelry of that unique night of the calendar year. For those who dress for the occasion to scare, playfully mock, perform pranks or just to entertain others; or who simply enjoy the merriment of the popular festivity, this night belongs to all of you at heart.

Hear the wind wailing and moaning at night, the loud knock on the front door and peek out the window to see who is waiting outside in the dark.
Boo!

PREFACE

Halloween conjures many thoughts in us – it has been recognised in various countries over the past few centuries as the solitary night of the year for trick or treating and dressing in macabre costumed disguises for special effect. However, its ancient Celtic beginnings as a pagan New Year celebration on the night of 31st October probably provides the most important basis for its many mysterious aspects.

It was at 'summer's end' in the Celtic calendar, when the onset of the powers of winter darkness were imminent; a night in which supernatural spirits temporarily returned to the world of the living. Conversely, the Christian commemoration of the dead subsequently introduced for the following day of 1st November – known as *All Saints' Day* – was far more sombre.

The unique festival of Halloween has many renditions and customs to attract participants; a festival of crop harvest and feasting, of unrestrained revelry, boisterous merriment, mischief-making and the wearing of ritualistic costumes to prevent being recognised by the hordes of returning spirits.

Shrieking phantasms, cackling witches, clanking skeletons and grinning demons, black cats, bats, ravens and creepy jack-o'-lanterns all play their respective roles in the festive time known as Halloween.

Maybe you prefer to convene your own Halloween party, or join the community costume parade in your local town, before heading out for some neighbourhood 'trick or treating' with fellow spirits. Enjoy the many ways to celebrate this ancient tradition, but be careful to select the right costume, lest you be mistaken for an actual supernatural spirit.

CONTENTS

LIST OF FIGURES	IV
THE MAGIK OF HALLOWE'EN	1
BONFYRES AND LANTERNS	6
PRANKING	12
PHANTASMS, WICCE AND DÆMONS	16
BOGIES AND BRETHEREN	24
HALLOWE'EN FAMILIARS	32
THE HALLOWE'EN PARTY	40
COSTUMED REVELRY	48
HALLOWE'EN SURPRISES	56
ALL HALLOWS' EVE	60
THE GRANDE PARADE	67
EPILOGUE	71
REFERENCES	74
BIBLIOGRAPHY	79
ABOUT THE AUTHOR	82

LIST OF FIGURES

Figure 1: All Hallows' Eve — 1
Figure 2: A Night of Merriment — 3
Figure 3: The Return of the Spirits — 5
Figure 4: The Hallowe'en Bonfire — 7
Figure 5: Gather in the Darkness — 8
Figure 6: Grotesque, Mischievous or Comical? — 9
Figure 7: Ample Stock on Hand — 11
Figure 8: Is that a Car on My Roof? — 13
Figure 9: Trick or Treat? — 15
Figure 10: Skeleton Pirates — 17
Figure 11: The Ultimate Decoration — 18
Figure 12: Ghost Choices — 19
Figure 13: Who is Knocking at My Door? — 20
Figure 14: Spells and Charms — 21
Figure 15: Hallowe'en Night — 22
Figure 16: Trio of Darkness — 25
Figure 17: The Graveyard Watcher — 28
Figure 18: Hallowe'en Scarecrows — 29
Figure 19: The Scarecrow — 31
Figure 20: The Ghost — 33
Figure 21: Swarming Bats — 34
Figure 22: Nocturnal Travellers — 35

Figure 23: Cat of Mystery or Shapeshifter?	36
Figure 24: Bird of Omen	38
Figure 25: The Hallowe'en Cemetery	41
Figure 26: Arachnids	41
Figure 27: The Harvest Festival	42
Figure 28: Petrified Mummies	43
Figure 29: Spider Cupcakes	43
Figure 30: Fudge Tombstones	44
Figure 31: What a Drink	45
Figure 32: Ghosts on the March	47
Figure 33: The Face behind the Mask	48
Figure 34: Hallowe'en Reveller	49
Figure 35: Supernatural Reveller	50
Figure 36: Scary or Humorous?	52
Figure 37: The Spectre	52
Figure 38: Cometh the Wicce	53
Figure 39: Light and Darkness	55
Figure 40: Spider Surprise	57
Figure 41: Glowing-Eye Raven	58
Figure 42: Phantom Revellers	61
Figure 43: The Witch Astride	64
Figure 44: The Gleaming Eyes	65
Figure 45: The Next King	66
Figure 46: This way to the Grand Parade	68
Figure 47: Come join the Parade	69
Figure 48: Enjoy the Festivity	71
Figure 49: A Festive Spirit	82

THE MAGIC OF HALLOWE'EN

Hallowe'en or Hallows' Eve – the annual festival of the harvest ('the feast of autumn') and commemoration of dead saints ('hallows') and other holy deceased – is celebrated in the month of October in a number of countries, culminating in the night of 31st October as the Eve of All Hallows Day.

The word evolved from a combination of *Hallow* and *e'en*; with the latter derived from Eve (*Even* in ancient dialect) and thus contracted to e'en [e(v) en], or simply een without the apostrophe.

Figure 1: All Hallows' Eve (© depositphotos)

In contemporary times, it is customary for people to adorn their dwellings with jack-o'-lanterns and various spectral decorations to ward off evil or malignant spirits. It is a time when the community visits seasonal outdoor attractions and Halloween-themed parks and haunt exhibits, engages in fairs and markets, convenes gigantic festive street parades with suitably costumed participants, or attends Hallowe'en parties and other rousing

HALLOWEEN SPIRITS

functions.

To provide an appropriate sense of perspective, imagine a two-storey, multi-room haunted house exhibit so large that it encompasses an area of almost 22, 000 square metres that takes 55 minutes to inspect, and employs over 150 personnel for the in-house Hallowe'en entertainment.[1] This can be found every October in Fort Worth Texas, and is the world's largest Hallowe'en exhibit.

For possibly the world's largest Hallowe'en party catering to costumed children and one of the largest in the USA, try the annual Hallowe'en party held in the 54 hectare grounds of the Louisville Zoo in Kentucky, USA. It has attracted around 90 000 guests each year.[2] The party is family-friendly and offers delight, cheer and merriment rather than frights and scares for all ages.

On Hallowe'en night, children, adolescents and the young-at-heart will disguise themselves ('guising') in dramatic fancy dress costumes representing a vast array of supernatural, mythological and other scary beasties, as well as famous or notorious fictional characters. It will be a night to frequent the streets, for pranking and in turn, receiving confectionary or pecuniary rewards, and for thorough enjoyment of the spirit of Hallowe'en.

Writer J.K.Bangs captures just such spirit in the poem *Hallowe'en* published in 1910:

> '...'Tis night when Goblin, Elf, and Fay [Fairy],
> Come dancing in their best array
> To prank and royster [boisterous frolic] on the way,
> And ease the troubled soul.
>
> The ghosts of all things, past parade,
> Emerging from the mist and shade
> That hid them from our gaze,
> And full of song and ringing mirth,
> In one glad moment of rebirth,
> Again they walk the ways of earth,
> As in the ancient days...'[3]

THE MAGIK OF HALLOWE'EN

Figure 2: A Night of Merriment (© depositphotos)

Writer Joel Benton portrayed yet another aspect to this celebration in his poem *Hallowe'en* produced some years earlier in 1896:

> 'Pixie, kobold [haunting spirit], elf, and sprite
> All are on their rounds to-night,—
> In the wan moon's silver ray

HALLOWEEN SPIRITS

> Thrives their helter-skelter play...
>
> ... Doors they move, and gates they hide
> Mischiefs that on moonbeams ride
> Are their deeds,—and, by their spells,
> Love records its oracles...'[4]

The ancestral history of Hallowe'en in its various forms has many names, and it is commonly accepted as having originated from the influence of early pagan rituals and festivities to honour the Sun. In particular, '... at the end of summer was a time of grief for the decline of the sun's glory, as well as a harvest festival of thanksgiving to him for having ripened the grain and fruit ...'[5]

The Celtic tribes (*Celtae*) who initially dominated central and western Europe from around 1200 B.C. to 500 B.C. were known for their paganistic deities and rites, which included sun worship. From this culture, we also have the languages of Irish, Scots, Welsh, Cornish and Gaelic amongst others, and each group has its own distinctive Hallowe'en customs and lore.

The ancient Celts recognised 'summer's end' on 31st October as the last day of the old year, and the vanquishing of the Sun for six months to the powers of winter darkness, aptly described by poet William Bryant in *The Death of the Flowers*:

> '... Of wailing winds, and naked woods, and meadows brown and sere [dry]. Heaped in the hollows of the grove, the wither'd leaves lie dead; ...
>
> ... The wind-flower and the violet, they perished long ago, And the wild rose and the orchis died among the summer glow:...'[6]

On that night, the ascendant powers of evil may return as spirits from abroad in various forms. These supernatural spirits were thought of as both the deceased and those who have never lived. The celebration of such spirits has many connotations dependent upon the country, including a night when the deceased or recently departed temporarily revisit the living.

THE MAGIK OF HALLOWE'EN

Folk would gather around the fire and make merry while the tempests of late autumn in October shrieked around like ghosts and demons on a mad carousel:

> 'The Autumn wind – oh hear it howl!
> Without – October's tempests scowl,
> As he troops away on the raving wind!
> And leaveth dry leaves in his path behind! …
>
> …'Tis the night, the night
> Of the grave's delight,
> And the warlocks are at their play! …
>
> …The spirits are pulling the sere dry leaves,
> Of the shadowy forest, down;
> And howl the gaunt reapers that gather the sheaves,
> With the moon, o'er their revels, to frown: …'[7]

Arthur Cleveland Coxe, *Hallowe'en, 1869*

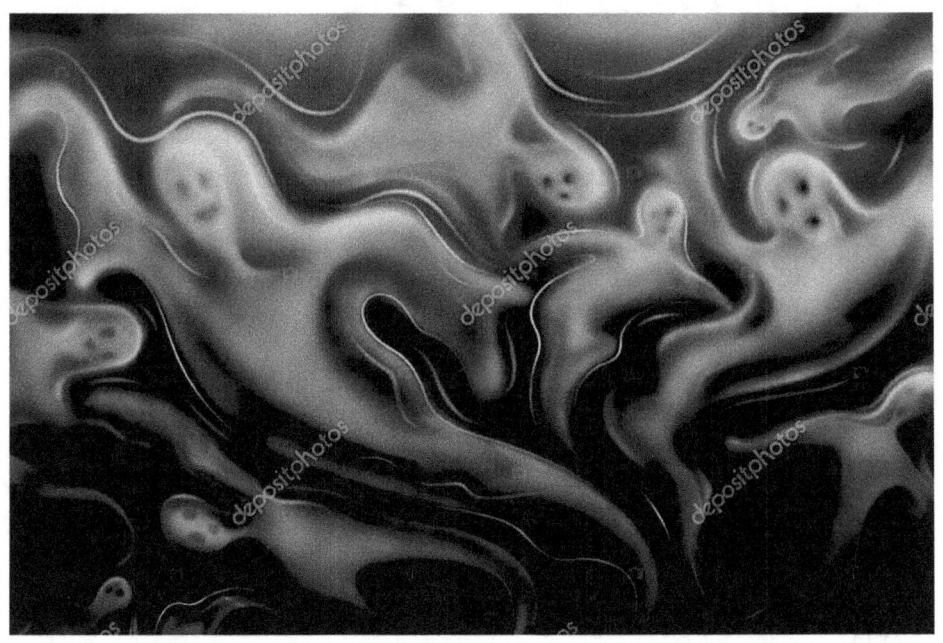

Figure 3: Return of the Spirits (© depositphotos)

BONFYRES AND LANTERNS

'...There is a world in which we dwell;
And yet a world invisible!
And do not think that naught can be,
Save only what with eyes ye see; ...'[1]

Coxe, *Hallowe'en, (1869)*

Almost everyone enjoys a substantial bonfire and for many centuries, this customary way to celebrate the Hallowe'en night of merriment and pranks prevailed. In recent generations, this custom has declined. The demise of such a ferocious symbolic spectacle possibly rests more with serious concerns for public safety and the likely risk of such a large fire getting out of control than with any neglect of this tradition.

Nonetheless, the term 'bonfire' for Hallowe'en is thought to be a relatively recent derivative of much older descriptions, such as *bone-fire* known as *bonefuyr* (ritualistic throwing of bones into the fire by pagan Celts and their priests, and during the Roman Empire), or *Bane-fire* (after a pagan deity named *Baal*).[2]

The Celtic bonfires played a significant role in Hallowe'en festivities and could be explained from one viewpoint as providing many benefits to their ancient rites – '... as tributes to the sun, as protection against evil spirits,

BONFYRES AND LANTERNS

and as beacons to friendly spirits returning home on Samhain; Gaelic for 'summer's end'; as well as marking the new year on 1st November.'[3]

Communal bonfires represented the nearest likeness to the Sun for the Celts, whilst providing the ideal means of thanksgiving for a bountiful harvest. There was also the additional benefit of protection from malicious spirits intent on causing mischief and mayhem. Stay within the perimeter of the bonfire to remain safe from any marauding beasties.

Figure 4: The Hallowe'en Bonfire (© Shutterstock)

The significant role of Hallowe'en bonfires throughout the British Isles is emphasised by the extreme variation in customs between the various locales, but a most effective use of fire was usually involved. Such bonfires (the flames, smoke and residual ashes) were considered by some to offer special beneficial powers, much like our Sun.

Blazing poles of bundled heath, broom or flax carried by villagers were a traditional staple to initiate the entire process and, in some cases, served as an additional protection against any possible marauding supernatural forces. Alternatively, when such torches were lit directly from a bonfire and taken around houses and fields, they could create yet another 'cleansing' layer of protection from evil spirits.

HALLOWEEN SPIRITS

With the massive bonfire underway, dancing around its boundary and not straying into the surrounding darkness were encouraged, with some enthusiastic participants occasionally choosing to leap over the flames at their peril.

These great bonfires represented a powerful symbol of the impending demise of summer and subsequent decay of crops, as well as providing a fiery blaze to deflect the onset of winter and its prevailing darkness; a province in which ghosts, demons and other supernatural beings thrived:

> 'Something betwixt heaven and hell,
> Something that neither stood nor fell.'
>
> **Scott,** *The Monastery, 1820*

Figure 5: Gather in the Darkness (© depositphotos)

BONFYRES AND LANTERNS

Bonfires were not the only prominent source of symbolic 'mystical fire' widely used for Hallowe'en. Candles and their use in lighting the interior of the popular Jack-o'-Lanterns (originally carved from turnips and other root vegetables and now from pumpkins) were also prolific.

Candles have been used as Hallowe'en luminaria since ancient times and that continues today. There are a customary way to illuminate and decorate a dwelling and its surrounds. The lighted candle transmits a warmth and glow very reminiscent of the Sun, and is commonly used as a poignant sign of remembrance of departed souls. When left burning in the windows of every room on Hallowe'en, they serve as guide for these wandering souls to return to the earthly homes of their families.

Figure 6: Grotesque, Mischievous or Comical? (© depositphotos)

HALLOWEEN SPIRITS

The Jack-o'- Lantern may appear to be simply a large hollowed-out vegetable with a grinning, fearsome or wicked expression, but the addition of a flickering candle within transforms the inanimate vegetable into something glowing and alive. Do they represent spirits or are they for frightening harmful spirits away?

'Jack of the lantern' originated in Britain in the 17th century, when such a phrase referred to any man carrying a lantern, or a night watchman, whose name was unknown (because folk used to called a man "Jack" if they didn't know his name). The appearance of a flickering glowing light (lantern) in the distance at night resembled the natural flame-like glow of phosphorescence caused by gases from decaying organic matter arising in marshes (*ignus fatuus*).[4]

The following excerpt from the poem *The Pumpkin* by American poet John Greenleaf Whittier published in 1849 provides an insight into jack-o'-lanterns:

> ' … When wild, ugly faces we carved in its skin,
> Glaring out through the dark with a candle within!
> When we laughed round the corn-heap, with hearts all in tune,
> Our chair a broad pumpkin,—our lantern the moon,
> Telling tales of the fairy who travelled like steam
> In a pumpkin-shell coach, with two rats for her team!'[5]

Folklore about the origins of Hallowe'en jack-o'-lanterns is diverse. However, the most common element in these tales is the displaying of lighted jack-o'-lanterns to frighten away spirits of the deceased and any supernatural demons roaming the night, thereby protecting dwellings and their inhabitants from these ethereal intruders.

On Hallowe'en night, when many costumed children and others celebrate the occasion, it may be difficult at times to discern between those masquerading and any potential spectres. Best to be prepared.

BONFYRES AND LANTERNS

Figure 7: Ample Stock on Hand (© depositphotos)

PRANKING

'... For, dressed as ghosts in purest white,
And horrid witches black as night,
We all went strolling here and there...'

Ada Clark, *My Wish (1930s)*

Hallowe'en pranking is the art of playing tricks on other people without causing any harm, humiliation, embarrassment, damage or destruction of property. It is a common custom to create mischief on Hallowe'en night and attribute the blame to malevolent spirits.

These tricks or practical jokes were intended to be humorous rather than hurtful, benevolent rather than spiteful, and are an integral part of the Hallowe'en tradition. Pranking should not be confused with the more contemporary salutation of 'trick or treating' that rapidly emerged in the mid -20th century in the USA which involves costumed participants moving through a neighbourhood house-to-house, knocking on front doors seeking confectionary and other treats and goodies.

Pranking is more related to the season of Hallowe'en, and can occur during associated parties or at any suitable time related to the prank. Its origins lie in those simpler bygone times when people were thoroughly entertained by storytelling, singing ballads or having their futures predicted (fortune-telling) at parties and other social gatherings.

Pranks ranged from the rather complicated disassembling of wagons and carriages and rebuilding them on top of barn roofs and cheeky substitution of cabbage leaves for washing on clotheslines, to tying front doors closed, removal of wagon wheels, and relocating various furniture, tools and ladders to awkward locations. For the more spirited revellers, the age-old pastime of egg-throwing remained very popular among adolescents.

Figure 8: Is that a Car on My Roof?

Pranking has progressively declined in the modern industrialised era, especially in the USA, where 'trick or treating' became increasingly popular amongst younger children, and as a result of destructive pranking incidents that went well beyond practical jokes. In some provinces, such activity was even consigned to the day before Hallowe'en – 30th October – known as Mischief Day.

Contemporary 'trick or treating' has retained some elements of pranking, including the custom of dressing in scary costumes to frighten away evil spirits such as demons and bogies. Trick or treating may have originated from the ancient Celtic mythology '… which included tales of supernatural beings demanding a tribute of food and drink on Samhain'[1], beginning at sunset on October 31st and continuing throughout the hours of darkness until the following dawn of the Celtic New Year.

The most rudimentary custom of this tradition was known as 'guising'

HALLOWEEN SPIRITS

when participants disguised in costumes which usually included a mask went door-to-door performing dances or other festive acts ('mumming'), reciting rhymes, recounting jokes or singing songs in return for rewards of food and drink. The wearing of such costumes at Hallowmas had been recorded in Scotland as far back as the 16th century.[2]

However, the phrase 'trick or treat' and its widespread popularity appears to be a relatively modern phenomenon of the 20th century, particularly as the practice involves a jocular threat in order to appease the tricksters.

The practical introduction of 'trick or treat' bags, buckets or hollow jack-o'-lanterns carried by participants served a dual purpose. Firstly, it was important to initially conceal any paraphernalia necessary to perform trickery, such as noisemakers, water pistols, rubber snakes and various oddments, in order to achieve the maximum shock effect.

One such example of a noisemaker device is called a *rattletrap*– a homemade device comprising a handle holding a star-shaped wheel. The wheel's frame had a thin spring leaf which struck the wheel repeatedly as the frame was quickly rotated around the wheel, '… creating a delightfully horrible racket…' for the ears.[3]

The second and more practical use of the bags, buckets and pumpkin heads was to contain the vast plunder of confectionary, cake, biscuits, nuts, other edible treats, small toys, trinkets and sometimes loose change offered by householders.

PRANKING

Figure 9: Trick or Treat? (© depositphotos)

To compensate for a lack of any planned tricks or threatened mischief, it is always wiser to dress in the most terrifying costume and be duly rewarded with treats instead.

PHANTASMS, WICCE AND DÆMONS

'...The candles are lighted, the hearthstones are swept,
The fires glow red.
We shall welcome them out of the night—
Our home-coming dead'.[1]

Winifred Letts, *Hallow E'en (1914)*

There are many symbolic costumes worn on Hallowe'en depicting entities that signify when 'the night rules'. These include skeletons and ghosts, which represent the souls of the departed. Witches and demons suggest the influence of the supernatural, magic, sorcery and paganistic rites.

There are also mythical beings of local folklore (goblins, bogies, imps), imaginative or fictional horror-figures (e.g. the Grim Reaper, banshees, mummies and scarecrows) and more recently, pirates – perhaps arising from the spectre of ghostly pirate ships and their traditional flag denoting the skull and crossbones.

PHANTASMS, WICCE AND DÆMONS

Figure 10: Skeleton Pirates (© depositphotos)

One of the most enduring Hallowe'en costumes is that of a ghostie – the phantasm of the deceased and quite an apparition to behold.

In the Celtic region of Brittany, it was believed that:

'Most of them stay not in some distant, definite Otherworld, but frequent the scenes of their former life. They never trespass upon daylight, and it is dangerous to meet them at night, … tell how the presence of a ghost made the midsummer air so cold that even wood did not burn …'[2]

Ghost costumes can be readily fabricated using bed sheets or pillow-cases and some careful crafting of eye-holes for better vision. For more elaborate versions, intricate accessories may be added, such as chains to rattle and clank, glow-in-the-dark colouration, and of course, wailing and groaning noises for additional optimum effect. A helium-filled party balloon or two beneath the draped sheet tends to create a floating *ghost* with unpredictable movements.

HALLOWEEN SPIRITS

Figure 11: The Ultimate Decoration (© depositphotos)

Now consider just how such a ghostly presence might be possible simply by using your imagination.

It was late autumn as the wind howled mournfully and relentlessly through leafless boughs, indicating the onset of an early winter was not far away. Even the sturdy wooden front door to the old farmhouse creaked loudly on its hinges, as if the wind was trying to enter through the cracks.[3]

Shortly before midnight as if upon some secret command, the tormented wind ceased ever so briefly. Total unearthly silence reigned inside and out, except for the intermittent crackling from the open fireplace as a half-burnt log collapsed into an ashen heap.

A sudden coldness in the night air became evident, and it was not due to standing on the cold stone floor of the farmhouse. The temperature had plummeted inside the farmhouse and the air became damp and stuffy as the clock on the wall chimed for midnight.

PHANTASMS, WICCE AND DÆMONS

Figure 12: Ghost Choices (© depositphotos)

Then, as if upon a further silent command, the wind resumed but not like before. It was pushing the front door as if someone or something was trying to enter. This large old door was well-made of solid oak and quite capable of withstanding even the strongest gusts of any passing tempest.

The door continued to vibrate violently and almost convulse as if under a force of massive pressure. Fortunately, it had been both locked and bolted for the night, so there was no risk that it may burst open. A low moaning sound accompanied this activity that made it seem like the wind itself was trying to communicate in some way.

The end to this cacophony of extreme structural shaking and mournful

HALLOWEEN SPIRITS

moaning came in a single dramatic moment best described by the loud noise made by slamming a door shut – a tremendous withering blast.

Whether it was the wind or something more ethereal attempting to enter the farmhouse after midnight is uncertain, but locking and bolting the door definitely stopped the inevitable entry by a powerful gale or the echoes of a severely disgruntled spirit trying to enter the portal.

Figure 13: Who is Knocking at My Door? (© depositphotos)

****

PHANTASMS, WICCE AND DÆMONS

Wicce ('witches') are possibly the most popular symbol of Hallowe'en after ghosts, and were commonly persecuted in grim ancient times for their association with the supernatural, divination of the Devil and various sacred rituals.

The superstitions of mythology and folklore often become intertwined, but for Hallowe'en, the presence of a witch astride a broomstick or indulging in sorcery and incantations appears a natural complement to the paganistic festive season of harvest.

Figure 14: Spells and Charms (© Shutterstock)

Add the various creatures known as 'witches' familiars' – such as black cats, bats, ravens, screech owls, wolves and toads – to this celebration, and it culminates in an impressive group of legendary Hallowe'en symbols.

In the stormy, blustery weather of late autumn, when wild winds were ideal for night-ridings by witches, could there be any more fearsome sight on a moonlight evening than the witch astride her broomstick venturing across the sky?

HALLOWEEN SPIRITS

English poet Robert Herrick provides a brief insight in the following part of his 1648 poem *The Hag*:

> 'The Hag is astride,
> This night for to ride;
> The Devill and shee together:
> Through thick, and through thin, ...
>
> ...Through Brakes [thickets] and through Bryars,
> O'er Ditches, and Mires,
> She followes the Spirit that guides now...'[4]

Figure 15: Hallowe'en Night (© depositphotos)

For those of us brave enough to travel widely on All Hallows' Eve, be vigilant of strangers because supernatural beings could also be out on this night.

One particular superstition beholds that witches are to be met at crossroads, and if '... one wishes to see witches, he must put on his clothes wrong side out, and creep backward to a crossroads, or wear wild radish ...'[5]. Strange things happen on Hallowe'en, including possibly even meeting a wicce.

****

PHANTASMS, WICCE AND DÆMONS

Hallowe'en costumes often portray demons, and these creatures represent the malicious spirits, considered by some to represent 'the sons of fallen angels and human mothers'. Where do such frightening creatures fit into this ancient celebration and why have such costumes remained so popular throughout Hallowe'en history?

If I were to offer plausible suggestions, it would be that demons are capable of creating malevolent mischief and have the right facial features to effectively scare people – 'light-up eyes', protruding horns, long sharp teeth, a fearful gaze and a bright colouration.

Such personal attributes must surely suit the antics of Hallowe'en perfectly. A bountiful crop harvest is probably the result of sufficiently favourable weather conditions, fertile ground and a lack of insect infestation – the opposite of the mayhem caused by those mischievous demons.

If one was to play a prank on a demon, simply lock all windows and doors to prevent it from entering your dwelling.

Ghouls are shapeshifting demons who were believed to frequent cemeteries or abandoned, uninhabited places. These are ravenous, malignant fiends intent on harassing and even devouring others, and hence are typically the last to leave any Hallowe'en celebration. They must be tightly controlled on Hallowe'en evening and never given the slightest opportunity to roam unsupervised without probable extreme consequences.

BOGIES & BRETHEREN

'They will sit where we sat, and will talk of us as we talked of them: in the gray of the morning only will they go away.'

Anatole Le Braz, *Night of the Dead (1893)*

The malicious or mischievous spirits that dominated olde world folklore, myths and legends have many names and descriptions, depending upon the country and local region. For the purposes of Hallowe'en, these entities may take several forms.

The bogie can be the most malicious and fiendish solitary spirit of them all, and possibly was the basis for the description 'the boogie-man' prevalent in childhood fairy tales. Bogles are the mischievous individual spirits that choose not to be malevolent or cause injury, whilst boggarts behave like poltergeists in their habits. The least frightening and most harmless of these spirits is the bug-a-boo; regarded more as a nursery bogie to scare children into good behaviour.[1]

In past centuries, when such tales of spirits were readily accepted based upon popular superstitions and ancient folklore, it could be common to celebrate the festivities of harvest dressed as a mischievous household goblin intent on pranking, a lumbering bogie with demonic glowing eyes, or maybe just as a sprightly imp of nature.

In the modern era of Hallowe'en, glowing eyes remain popular but shrouded inside long draping cloaks to suggest an image of an unknown spirit of darkness.

Figure 16: Trio of Darkness (© depositphotos)

So, if adventurous enough to spend Hallowe'en night travelling between parties, it is probably wise to disguise oneself to fool any stray wandering spirit encountered.

It is said dressing in religious saintly costume may deceive them from recognising you, but if the wanderer happens to be a marauding goblin, you may need the assistance of 'the protectors of the corn harvest':

'On Hallowe'en the gobble-uns

HALLOWEEN SPIRITS

>May seize and carry you off to their den;
>So you'd best try hard to obtain the guard
>Of Kernel Corn and his husk-y men.'[2]

****

On Hallowe'en night the bretheren of the graveyard are other spirits to be avoided wherever practicable. They come in many haunting shapes; some with a decidedly malevolent attitude and others with a fixation on teasing the living.

The Banshee female spirit is often depicted as a messenger of death in local folklore in Ireland, although is not a prominent presence in Hallowe'en lore.[3] She has also been known as the 'Angel of Death' or the 'White Lady of Sorrow'.

When described in Hallowe'en fairy tales, two significant features of appearance and sound remain consistent: the Banshee is traditionally cloaked in an unusual gown, robe or hood and has '…unnaturally long hair and a corpse-like pallor'.[4] The Banshee not only wails mournfully and incessantly, but has been known to release a terrifying, deafening shriek when confronted.

The mournful wail is a sound said to resemble the melancholy moaning of the wind –

>'… Anon she pours a harrowing strain,
>And then she sits all mute again!
>Now peals the wild funereal cry,
>And now – it sinks into a sigh'.[5]

For those contemplating Hallowe'en as a costumed Banshee, it would be mandatory to have a suitably high pitched voice capable of an utterly piercing screech on request. For a realistic appearance, the Banshee must resemble nothing belonging to this world. It should have a queer-shaped, gleaming face with a hellish expression, and generate sheer horror in those around her – quite an accomplishment on Hallowe'en, given the many others in scary costumes.

BOGIES AND BRETHEREN

One redeeming feature of this choice of costume is that anyone who hears, sees or is aware of the Banshee is immune from its prognostication of impending death, as it never manifests itself directly to the unfortunate doomed one yet to perish[6], and that must be a great relief for any party-goer.

If the sight of such a startling spectre is too realistic, another way to shock any Hallowe'en party is to invite the phantom door-knocker that is heard yet never seen.

In bygone times, most front doors had metal hinged knockers to alert the householders of a visitor. On one particular evening, the door knocker was loudly rapped but when the front door was opened, there was no-one there. Shortly afterwards, the same process recurred and still there was no-one present at the front door.

The householder became annoyed and crept to one of side windows to observe the door-knocker, only to receive a shock: 'The full light of the moon fell on the door, and as he [householder] looked, the knocker was again lifted and loudly rapped.'[7] This had to be a portent of impending death in the household.

A less menacing but more familiar spectre that frequents Hallowe'en, and is known as the King of Terror, is the Grim Reaper or the Graveyard Watcher. What a sight to behold!

HALLOWEEN SPIRITS

Figure 17: The Graveyard Watcher (© depositphotos)

BOGIES AND BRETHEREN

This mythical apparition traditionally carries a scythe like those used by harvesters to reap or harvest their crops, and during the Hallowe'en season, may be a customary visitor to associated parties to reap the maximum mayhem/divine harvest. In the guise of a Graveyard Watcher, it remains silent but certainly has a remarkable front seat view to ghostly activities:

> '…The dead all arose from their sleeping,
> Round the tombs grimly dancing and leaping.
> In a skeleton ring, then, together they hung,
> While they danced as the waves of the ocean …
> …But their grave-clothes hindered their motion; …
>
> …At last it was o'er, and the skeleton crowd,
> One after another, each slipped on its shroud;
> Then into their cold graves they glided,
> And silence once more presided'.[8]

Scarecrows or 'harvest figures' warrant consideration in association with Hallowe'en, although their original function to protect crops from flocks of scavenging birds is not necessarily practical in late autumn following the completion of harvest.

However, these solitary symbols of defiance perched precariously in the middle of a paddock can offer far more at Hallowe'en than simply preserving crops from predators.

Figure 18: Hallowe'en Scarecrows (© depositphotos)

HALLOWEEN SPIRITS

Most people would consider a scarecrow as a motionless, silent sentinel standing in a pasture with arms dramatically extended horizontally in a vain effort to frighten birds, but instead only providing these pesky creatures with a comfortable perch from which to observe the crops below at closer quarters.

Some innovative farmers even fabricate their scarecrows with stark, gaunt body shapes and position them with a threatening stance, adding a menacing facial expression as a final touch, but all to no avail.

However, on Hallowe'en night, these lonely figures can be majestically transformed with some deft changes to their appearance. One common practice is to substitute grinning jack-o'-lanterns for their heads, endowing them with a decidedly eerie look.

For three young boys taking a short-cut across just such a paddock on a rural property early on Hallowe'en night, it turned out to be quite a journey. The local farmer had made some minor modifications to his solitary resident scarecrow on the previous day.

As the trio approached the stationary scarecrow in the distance, they observed in the darkness that it seemed to be occasionally moving its arms, yet there was no discernible breeze on this relatively calm and moonless night. As they got closer, the boys also noticed that the scarecrow appeared to have grown alarmingly, to about 2.5 metres in height, and its eyes were actually glowing.

Upon reaching the 'scarecrow', the nervous boys were now confronted by what appeared to be a ghostly spectre with supernatural eyes and whose arms where waving up and down with thin skeletal fingers gesturing wildly. This is the precise moment when fright turned into uncontrollable panic and the trio fled without looking back.

The following morning when the boys returned to the property, they were enlightened by the farmer who shared his practical joke with them. He had become weary of local children traversing his paddocks at night and decided to modify his scarecrow just for this one special evening.

BOGIES AND BRETHEREN

First, he added a large and spindly leafless branch to substantially increase the height and size of the scarecrow and covered the body in lightweight white hessian to resemble a ghostly shroud. By tightly intertwining the fabric around the scarecrow 'arms' of the branch, it was possible for them to move freely with the slightest air movement. The sticks protruding from the ends of these arms then looked like gaunt fingers.

Glowing otherworldly eyes were achieved by careful placement of special bioluminescent fungi found locally in decaying wood and on rotting bark. These fungi generate a natural blueish-green dim glow at night, known as 'fox (false) fire'.[9]

The Hallowe'en phantom scarecrow had been successful in frightening those taking a short-cut across this paddock, but it would resume its customary duties after this night.

Figure 19: The Scarecrow (© depositphotos)

HALLOWE'EN FAMILIARS

'...Ha! They are on us, close without!
Shut tight the shelter where we lie!
With hideous din the monster rout,
Dragon and vampire, fill the sky!...'[1]

Victor Hugo, *The Djinns (1829)*

The most familiar airborne creature to dominate the night on Hallows' Eve is probably the bat, and there many species throughout the world. One of more unusual and amongst the rarest is the Australian Ghost Bat (*Macroderma gigas*), or false vampire bat.

This character is relatively large in size and its 'wings' are of such an extremely thin membrane that it appears almost ghostly at night when in flight.[2] They also have very large ears for improved hearing, exceptional vision and particularly sharp teeth which are ideal attributes for any bat, especially on Hallowe'en night.

Bats have some special features, including being the only mammals capable of truly sustained flight (by having forelimbs adapted as 'wings'), unlike others that tend to glide.[3] In the Americas, the common vampire bats only feed on animal blood of large mammals and so should be prudently avoided, particularly during the sleeping hours.

HALLOWE'EN FAMILIARS

Figure 20: The Ghost (© depositphotos)

In many cultures, including in Europe, bats are associated with darkness, death, witchcraft and malevolence.[4] Such associations are common with the nocturnal traditions encountered on Hallowe'en.

For anyone who has ever encountered the migration of thousands upon thousands of bats departing caves or forests at twilight, the sight is overwhelming to say the least. Fortunately, this is not a feature of the harvest celebration, except for fruit-devouring bats of course.

These megabats have a wingspan up to 1.7 metres, consume mostly ripe fruit, nectar and pollen, and can fly significant distances in a single night.

HALLOWEEN SPIRITS

Figure 21: Swarming Bats (© depositphotos)

For those celebrating on Hallowe'en night, it is best to avoid 'any streaming swarm on a storm of dark wings' by staying under cover, or endure the consequences as suggested in the following prose from *The Djinns* by Hugo:

> '...Wild cries of hell! voices that howl and shriek!
> The horrid swarm before the tempest tossed –
> O'Heaven! – descends my lowly roof to seek:
> Bends the strong wall beneath the furious host.
> Totters the house, as though, like dry leaf shorn
> From autumn bough and on the mad blast borne,
> Up from its deep foundations it were torn
> To join the stormy whirl, Ah, all is lost!...'[5]

HALLOWE'EN FAMILIARS

Figure 22: Nocturnal Travellers (© depositphotos)

****

Whilst the bat appears to be the dominant force in the night skies, the spooky yet humble black cat is surely the most recognisable Hallowe'en animal on the ground:

'In medieval Europe, the cat was often considered an emblem of evil whose glowing eyes not only penetrate darkness but also glimpse a sinister other world: an omen of bad luck, even a messenger of the devil. As the supposed cohorts of witches and demons, cats were regarded as agents of dark powers and nameless horrors.'[6]

At Hallowe'en, the black cat has the rare opportunity for redemption from the myths surrounding their association with witchcraft and the superstitions about causing bad luck and personal misfortune fostered throughout history.

HALLOWEEN SPIRITS

Figure 23: Cat of Mystery or Shapeshifter? (© depositphotos)

In some parts of the world, it is firmly believed that such cats actually bring good luck and are omens of significantly improved life and prosperity. For the ancient Egyptians, cats were revered and afforded the greatest respect.[7] In Celtic culture, the cat was considered sacred by the Druid priests and 'a slender black cat reclining on a chain of old silver' guarded treasure.[8]

The black cat's reputation is as a potential shapeshifter of a human transformed by sorcery into a feline, and it is thought to possess various supernatural traits that make it most suitable for the Hallowe'en season; when the ethereal spirits from the other world revisit the living.

Of all cats on the planet, the coal-black to greyish black version without discernible markings certainly provides the right mystique of strangeness with a distinctive aura of the supernatural to suit such a celebration.

HALLOWE'EN FAMILIARS

Unfortunately, the pigmentation eumelanin which causes their black fur can also fade – fading becoming more pronounced where frequently exposed to sunlight – causing black cats to "rust" to a lighter brownish shade[9], in spite of their supernatural talents and powers.

The jack-o'-lantern may sit '…on the throne as the undisputed king of Halloween icons,'[10] but it is the black cat and 'the ancient popular notion which regarded all such cats as witches in disguise'[11] that propelled these into classic symbols of Hallowe'en.

Perhaps the basis for the popularity of this domesticated feline during this season might actually be found in a cat's inherent abilities to appear (or disappear) without any particular reason or need. Cats tend to do the unexpected and sometimes turn-up in rather odd locations when selecting a comfortable place to sleep or if seeking shelter. They may crave your company at one moment and then ignore your attentions thereafter. These enigmatic elements of unusual behaviour add to their mystique, particularly when the cat is black.

****

> '…Ghastly grim and ancient raven wandering from the Nightly shore – …
> … What this grim, ungainly, ghastly, gaunt and ominous bird of yore …'[12]

These lines taken from the famous 1845 poem *The Raven* by American writer Edgar Allan Poe suggest the essential supernatural and mysterious spirit attributable to this enigmatic bird.

Ravens were respected in various ancient cultures and represented in their mythologies and folklore as highly intelligent, clever and bold in nature. Their unusual ability to predict the onset of one's death by exhibiting weird behaviour and/or making exotic noises endowed ravens with quite a fearsome reputation.[13]

What sets the raven apart is the distinctively hoarse, croaking voice from its guttural throat, rather than the high pitched, raucous calls of so many other

HALLOWEEN SPIRITS

birds. It is almost a dignified voice.

Figure 24: Bird of Omen (© depositphotos)

Ravens have always been recognised as companions of witches, enhancing the performance of witchcraft magic through their superior intelligence and providing a means for astral travel between destinations. They were thought to have acted as messengers by collecting information for witches and by spreading the magic across great distances at night, when their all-black gloomy plumage was virtually undetectable in the sky.[14]

Their presence at Hallowe'en provides the celebration with a sense of foreboding that something ominous might occur.

HALLOWE'EN FAMILIARS

The ferocious Vikings embraced the sacred raven symbol as their 'Bird of Omen' in preference to all other creatures – it ultimately came to be known as a bird of evil omen across much of western Europe. This gloomy messenger that '…became associated with images of death and despair'[15], of bad tidings and evil, is aptly suited to attend the Hallowe'en party.

THE HALLOWE'EN PARTY

...Eye of newt, and toe of frog,
Wool of bat, and tongue of dog,
Adder's fork, and blindworm's sting,
Lizard's leg, and owlet's wing, ...

William Shakespeare, *Macbeth (1606)*

There are many elements to convening a successful Hallowe'en party, and one crucial requirement is to assemble the most convincing decorations. When deciding the overall theme of the event, it is best to select a popular theatrical setting for the background layout.

If the emphasis is upon the unearthly and the grim, a cemetery setting with plenty of polystyrene tombstones, stone carvings of sculptured gothic faces, plastic skeletons, burning lanterns and perhaps a fake coffin and the grim reaper in costume would suffice. This could be complemented by an artificial fog to create a haunting atmosphere.

For a haunted dwelling, the introduction of copious numbers of fake spiders hanging in webs, including a few large arachnids, as well as many rubber flying bats strung from suitable elevated positions is probably more appropriate.

THE HALLOWE'EN PARTY

Figure 25: The Hallowe'en Cemetery (© depositphotos)

Figure 26: Arachnids

HALLOWEEN SPIRITS

Figure 27: The Harvest Festival (© depositphotos)

****

What is a Hallowe'en party without an appropriate feast of treats and confectionary? There should be a grand supper fit for the visiting array of guests; ghosts and ghouls, witches and wizards, shapeshifters and skeletons, demons and bogies, sprites and pirates, and other spirits roaming through the party.

For a tasty appetiser, perhaps start the evening with entangled mummies masquerading as stuffed capsicum ('peppers') under serious attack by marauding plastic spiders.

THE HALLOWE'EN PARTY

Figure 28: Petrified Mummies (© depositphotos)

Who does not like cupcakes and the sweet icing topping each treat? The Hallowe'en spider version might just appeal to those with a discerning eye for the unusual.

Figure 29: Spider Cupcakes (© depositphotos)

HALLOWEEN SPIRITS

Slices of baked chocolate fudge with lettering of frosted icing should appeal to the sweet tooth in most of us. They have also been prepared with a distinctive Hallowe'en theme.

Figure 30: Fudge Tombstones (© depositphotos)

No party would be complete without refreshing beverages, and for this special occasion, how about something almost out of this world and into the next? If it needs a name, try 'Creature Feature'.

THE HALLOWE'EN PARTY

Figure 31: What A Drink (© depositphotos)

****

Hallowe'en parties need spooky fun and spirited dances to entertain the gathering of creepy guests, and what better than the entertaining Witches' Dance to cast some magic into the night's festivities.

Such a dance is performed by eight costumed witches complete with their broomsticks, and may be either brief or prolonged depending upon their theatrical stamina.

All the volunteer witches enter astride their brooms and slowly dance in a circle, first in one direction, then reversing in opposite directions whilst constantly hissing. Next they form a long line and all whirl their broomsticks in the air followed by more hissing. This progresses into clumping the broomstick handles together three times and meowing like cats.

HALLOWEEN SPIRITS

The hissing and meowing grows progressively louder as the dance proceeds and the witches pass each other whirling the brooms, dancing around the stationary brooms and leering, dragging them across the floor or clumping the handles together. As a finale, all the witches depart the dance by riding the brooms out of sight of party guests whilst still hissing loudly. Naturally, the accompanying music must be suitably supernatural in tone.[1]

Excerpts from the extensive poem *Broomstick Train; or Return of the Witches* by Oliver Wendell Holmes Sr. provided as a recitation would add further suspense to this Hallowe'en festivity:

> '…On their well-trained broomsticks mounted high.
> Seen like shadows against the sky;
> Crossing the tracks of owls and bats,
> Hugging before them their coal-black cats…
>
> … No sooner the withered hags were free
> Than out they swarmed for a midnight spree;…
>
> …They came, of course, at their master's call,
> The witches, the broomsticks, the cats, and all;…'[2]

For those enjoying the night with spooky ghosts and spectres, the performance of the 'Spook March' should send a chill through your bones. In this enactment, all guests dressed as ghosts converge into one area whilst revolving their heads, waving arms up and down, and '… moaning, groaning and walking as if lost'.

Having formed into a single line, all ghosts then start to retreat, peering and pointing ominously at remaining guests, and then moaning deeply before moving in circle, shaking their heads sideways and waving their arms. Further encounters with the watching guests revive more frightful groans and hissing.

All the ghosts move to separate locations and then '… rush groaning and moaning from these corners … with both arms at face level pointing' at the guests. They reverse to their original positions before re-forming in a single line, complete with various swaying motions and further moaning.

THE HALLOWE'EN PARTY

The march finishes with all ghosts uttering awful moans.[3]

No accompanying music is necessary as the persistent ghostly utterances suffice to entertain the assembled guests.

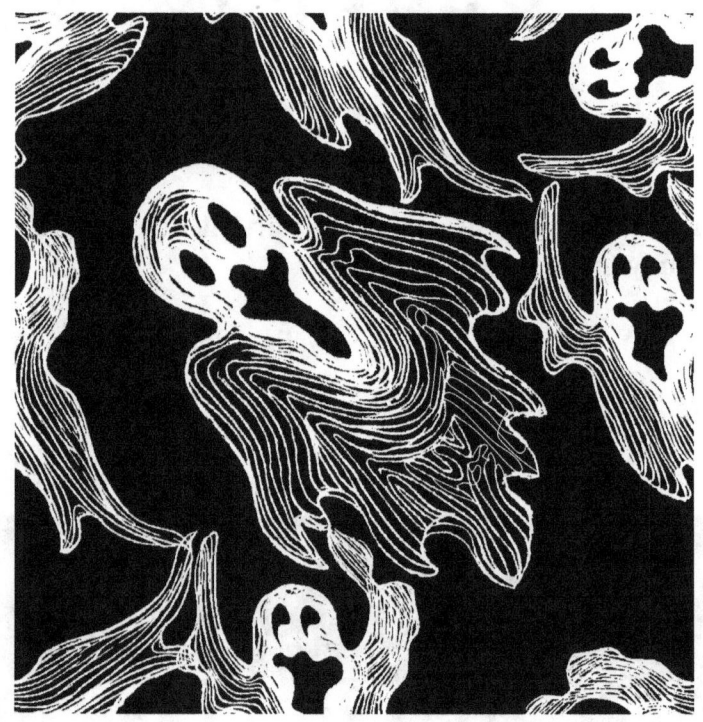

Figure 32: Ghosts on the March (© depositphotos)

'… Doors they move, and gates they hide
Mischiefs that on moonbeams ride …

…Eery shadows were they then —
But to-night they come again;…[4]

COSTUMED REVELRY

'There are nights when the wolves are silent and only the moon howls.' [1]

                George Carlin, *Brain Droppings (1997)*

Figure 33: The Face behind the Mask (© Shutterstock)

COSTUMED REVELRY

For those hardy souls celebrating the Hallowe'en night, expect a prolonged night of revelry and merriment, of camaraderie and friendship, and of meeting new people. It is said that the costume maketh the person, and there are certainly many choices available.

There are no favourite or elective costumes for this special night, but there are still some fundamental rules to appreciate. For trick-or-treating and dispensing the Hallowe'en message, the optimum choice of costume is to appear scary without being overtly frightening.

Your choice of treats becomes severely limited if the householder adamantly refuses to open the door to a terrifying visitor from the supernatural. For those trick-or-treaters travelling in a group, it is always wise to mix'n match costumes and for everyone to dress differently. Too many pumpkin heads only cause confusion.

Dragging ghostly shrouds, witches' capes and other spooky paraphernalia around can become exhausting, especially when also lugging overladen sacks/buckets of treats. Patience and perseverance are crucial to an enjoyable night for all. The most important rule of all is to enjoy the special night.

Figure 34: Hallowe'en Reveller (© depositphotos)

HALLOWEEN SPIRITS

Street parades celebrating this festival have become common across the Western world, with attendances approaching 50,000 people in some major cities. Each city designates a specific theme for their celebrations and participants are encouraged to dress to match these themes. Such parades are almost always accompanied by groups of musicians providing the essential merriment to each parade.

The New Orleans celebration in Louisiana, USA, is a spooktacular Hallowe'en street parade. It may not be the largest parade in the country, but it is held in the city widely known as 'The Most Haunted City in America', thus providing a most suitable setting for Hallowe'en.

Figure 35: Supernatural Reveller (© depositphotos)

COSTUMED REVELRY

The grand Hallowe'en parade is convened in its historic French Quarter, an area with extensive history and ancient culture associated with mystical spiritual practices. The French Quarter readily embraces the Hallowe'en celebration with extraordinary decorations and elaborate lighting to provide an additional mystical enhancement to crowd festivities.

It is a perfect venue for a massive street party with all its revelry and ghostly fun activity. It even provides great vantage points well above street level, enabling spectators to share a panoramic view of the communal celebrations underway below.

The two most common celebratory elements now associated with Hallowe'en in the modern era are 'night' and 'death'. It is no longer a celebration of the crop harvest as in bygone times. These days participants of this tradition are more likely to select their costumes based upon beings from the spiritual darkness or fearsome night-dwellers who thrived in the hours before dawn, or in some other way represent death – think skeletons, vampyres, ghouls and other nasties.

Although these selections may appear rather sombre and grim, Hallowe'en is also about having fun and enjoying the moment. With this in mind, I select my ideal costumes to effectively illustrate this unusual tradition.

There are various terms to describe a ghost – phantasm, spectre, apparition or spiritual manifestation to name a few – and there have probably been a vast range of ghosts sighted throughout our human history.

The depiction of such an ethereal spirit at Hallowe'en is also common, and in many ways, is the best way to clearly announce that 'the spirits have returned to the living for just this peculiar night'. The ghost image portrays the stark contrast between the living and the deceased. Trick-or-treating on Hallowe'en night provides an avenue for them to return – it gives them a temporary refuge amongst the living. The ghostly visitor is possibly the simplest costume to fabricate yet can also portray a powerful presence appearing at your door on a dark night.

HALLOWEEN SPIRITS

Figure 36: Scary or Humorous? (© depositphotos)

Figure 37: The Spectre (© depositphotos)

COSTUMED REVELRY

What classic figure is associated with perceived supernatural powers to cast spells, predict the future, influence nature's elements, fly astride various objects or animals, and accomplish numerous other extraordinary feats? The witch, so often depicted in the ancient times as being '...of flowing black cloaks, pointed hats and chins, warty noses, flying broomsticks, and steaming cauldrons' [2], symbolises Hallowe'en night.

The witch costume consists of entirely black apparel and a straw or flax broomstick, but it is also crucial to include some familiars. An ominous raven perched on one shoulder and a slinky black cat clasped under one arm should provide the necessary supernatural charm.

Figure 38: Cometh the Wicce (© depositphotos)

HALLOWEEN SPIRITS

Aside from the traditionally recognised costumes for Hallowe'en night, there are also the ubiquitous mythological outfits. These can be simply a product of one's vivid imagination or based upon legendary or fictional sources. Some people elect to be demons and creepy pumpkin characters, others transform into primordial beasties, whilst yet others settle for mysterious hooded haunts.

The character selected is not important, so long as the costume befits the image, and the choices are vast.

> 'The dance between darkness and light will always remain –
> the stars and the moon will always require the darkness to be seen, the darkness will just not be worth having without the stars and the moon.'
>
> **C.Joybell C., American Writer**

COSTUMED REVELRY

Figure 39: Light and Darkness (© depositphotos)

HALLOWE'EN SURPRISES

Ghosts of the Twentieth Century:
Fellow Ghosts -- Assemble in the cellar and then rise.
Spirits will please check their wraps.
Ghosts of ideas must be well labelled, or they will be carried out.
All banshees, ghouls, will-o'-the-wisps, genii, and other old-time apparitions, are politely requested to absent themselves.
Astral bodies must be wrapt in more than thought...[1]

Vintage Hallowe'en Invitation Form (1903)

In bygone times, before the advent of modern technological conveniences like television, computers, mobile phones and satellites, Hallowe'en entertainment was largely provided by attending masquerade parties and group participation in an array of festivities.

It was not unusual to reward guests attending such parties for their garish costumes, ranging from the scariest and most daunting to the most innovative and highly thoughtful outfits.

These parties traditionally involved numerous fanciful games, imaginative competitions to test one's capabilities – such as ducking for apples, simple water experiments or shadow pantomimes – and elaborate mysterious tests with a distinctively humorous Hallowe'en theme. Such a test may have been randomly selecting a passage from a book of spells and charms; guests' attempts to mimic the spell or charm process usually produced unusual and enlightening outcomes.

HALLOWE'EN SURPRISES

The reward for successfully completing select contests in those days (and not being turned into a black cat as well) was almost always a distinctive souvenir of Hallowe'en – a reminder of the great evening. These included charm items depicting witches, ghosts, bats or select pieces of quirky fruit or vegetables representing the harvest crop – pineapples, coconuts or cobs of corn. However, the special prizes of the night were the highly valued 'secret' rewards for the most impressive Hallowe'en costumes, and for these gems, I refer to some direct modern experiences.

The mystery shoe-box prize is almost always keenly sought, if not just for the novelty of discovering what it actually contains. The prize needs to be intricately wrapped in several layers of fine tissue paper and then further enclosed in brown paper tightly wrapped with twine to ensure it is completely obscured in shape and size.

As the prize-winner finally peeled off the last layer of paper, not only was the secret revealed as a gigantic synthetic Tarantula spider with multiple quivering hairy legs, but the prize and the shoe-box were instantly thrown into the air. In fact, that now airborne artificial spider cleared a swathe through the surrounding guests for about a ten metre radius as sheer blind panic ensued. Fortunately, the realistic imitation did not land on anyone and that was quite a relief for all concerned. Now for the next prize ...

Figure 40: Spider Surprise

HALLOWEEN SPIRITS

The next prize was also rather unexpected as it was not a wriggling intertwined mangle of rubber snakes nor a mechanical bat, but something far more subdued. For a start, it was inanimate and not alive. The lucky guest cautiously celebrated winning the party prize for a great costume by gingerly handling the package.

After unwrapping the several layers of surgical gauze enveloping the object, it was soon revealed as something soft, rubbery and limp – in true Hallowe'en fashion, it turned out to be a fake hand made entirely of silicon with its fingers configured in a clutching grasp. It was also covered in glow-in-the-dark paint. The winner decided to leave it on the nearest table for other guests to admire from a distance.

Another less elaborate prize is still certainly suitable for this supernatural night – an artificial large black raven with red glowing eyes that can perch comfortably on your shoulder. It is perfect as a companion for you at the party, and it croaks intermittently as well as flashing those red glaring eyes upon command.

Figure 41: Glowing-Eye Raven (© depositphotos)

HALLOWE'EN SURPRISES

Surprise gifts for Hallowe'en costumes do not always have to be scary or creepy, but they can be unexpected.

In the early 20th century, Hallowe'en-themed celebrations were still representative of ancient merrymakings, with all-night revelry and costume parties convened to keenly preserve the strange and mystifying traditions of the past:

'For parties held in private houses, secrecy ruled. No one told anyone else they were invited and guests came disguised, wearing masks and dressed up as ghosts, witches, goblins, or anything else deemed appropriate.'[2]

The secrecy of each party ensured all guests could maintain total anonymity and thus preserve a mystique about each other, only identifying themselves if so choosing to unmask. The entertainment was both in guessing who may be each costumed figure, and the surprise in discovering later in the evening someone entirely different.

An elaborate celebratory disguise in those times might also require playing your character – be it ghost, pirate or witch – for the night.

ALL HALLOWS'EVE

'…Sometimes they're in the corner, sometimes they're by the door,
Sometimes they're all a-standin' in the middle uv [of] the floor;
Sometimes they are a-sittin' down, sometimes they're walkin' round
So softly an' so creepy-like they never make a sound;
Sometimes they are as black as ink, an' other times they're white.
But the color ain't no difference when you see things at night! …'[1]

Eugene Field, *Seein' Things (1894)*

What of the mystical elements attributed to All Hallows' Eve and the various lores and tales shared throughout various parts of the world? American poet and humourist Eugene Field, who was also known as the 'Poet of Childhood' for his light-hearted poems, certainly embraced a child's perspective of seeing 'things' at night.

Hallows' Eve is a peculiar night of the year '…said to be the time when the veil between this world and the next [the afterlife] is stretched the thinnest'[2], and the spirits of the dead are all stirring. A time of final opportunity for unfortunate souls of the departed to seek out the living still in the material world before moving on to the afterlife.

A time possibly for witches, spirit familiars and devils masquerading as ghosts to temporarily dance together in great merriment and unholy revelry.

For those who had imprudently stayed out very late on such an evening, it could also be possible to keep company with the dead without realising it.

ALL HALLOWS' EVE

In a supernatural tale recounted in the ancient legends of Ireland, one such young man enjoying the merriment that evening fell in with a group of strange revellers who encouraged him to join their festivities.

As the revellers danced around him, they laughed loudly and encouraged him to join them by taking his hands.

Figure 42: Phantom Revellers (© depositphotos)

However, upon closer inspection of any one of them, the young man recognised each was a friend who had either died in the past year or a long time ago – '…all the dancers, men, women, and girls, were the dead in their long, white shrouds'. Trying to escape was pointless as the ghostly dancers 'coiled' around him, gripping his arms and attempting to relentlessly draw the young man into the dance, whilst shrieking with laughter.[3]

He resisted their efforts until falling senseless on the ground, only awaken-

HALLOWEEN SPIRITS

ing the following morning with his arms covered in black marks from the touch of the hands of the dead.

The young man had been mocked and punished for disturbing the spirit revels on the November Eve –

> '…that one night of all the year when the dead can leave their graves and dance in the moonlight on the hill, and mortals should stay at home and never dare to look upon them'.[4]

If someone has to confront wild supernatural spirits before midnight on All Hallows' Eve, then it is preferable to do so with a friend. For a farmer and his labourer/servant in a remote, wind-swept and hilly region of Lancashire in the late 19th century, this was to be the case.

The farmer, his family and their servant shared a small, lonely cottage located near the base of a massive, flat-topped hill well known for its majestic views of the surrounding lands, its treacherous ravines, and for its notorious history as a secretive gathering place for witches.

At the summit of this great hill was an unusual tower in which, according to local superstition, unholy, weird and demonic acts of evil revelry were thought to occur.

In this isolated rural setting, with few neighbours within a mile, the farmer experienced some peculiar personal hardships following a frightful gloomy night when the wind moaned, howled and shrieked 'almost wickedly'. These included the sudden inexplicable sickness of his children, the subsequent death of one child as well as some of his livestock, and blighted crops.[5]

The farmer became convinced that '…he had in some unknown way incurred the displeasure of the invisible powers …',[6] and that this required some direct action be taken against these supernatural fiends.

One superstitious ceremony known to the farmer was *lighting the witches*. This involved carrying a lighted candle about the local hills between 11 p.m. and midnight to overcome the evil powers of witches who would try their utmost to extinguish its flame. Even if the candle was inadvertently

ALL HALLOWS' EVE

extinguished, it still represented an evil omen.[7]

The farmer was also aware that 'others had lighted the witches' previously and achieved a prolonged immunity from their malicious influences.

This meant confronting the coven with lighted candles on Hallows' Eve when they would be perhaps most vulnerable, thereby preventing their powers becoming any stronger. To provide further protection for the farmer and his servant, each took a branch of mountain ash tied with several sprigs of bay to safely ward off thunder, lightning and any stray fiends encountered.[8]

The area was subject to wild weather at times, with fierce tempests and accompanying lightning bolts and deafening thunder claps. Although the last day of October was cloudy with a misty rain, by nightfall the rain had ceased and a light wind prevailed.

At 10 p.m. that evening, the two men approached the hill with lighted candles and branches of mountain ash in hand, accompanied by the loyal farm dog for company. By the time they reached the foot of the hill near a well-known ravine, the wind had 'ceased to whisper', leaving them to commence the climb in ominous silence.

Just before reaching the top of this ravine, the men were suddenly jolted by a violent flash of lightning and a thunderous clap of thunder as a storm approached. However, it was not the impending inclement weather that frightened them, but rather '… the weird and unearthly shriek of laughter … as a black figure flew slowly past them, almost brushing against their faces in flight'.[9]

HALLOWEEN SPIRITS

Figure 43: The Witch Astride (© depositphotos)

This resulted in the farm dog immediately fleeing whilst howling terribly. Now there was only the two of them remaining to confront the fiends, but at least their candles were still alight.

They trudged on relentlessly, over the rough stony ground, without any further mishap until within site of the tower at the summit, before encountering quite a sight.

The tower's windows were illuminated and every so often, a dark figure was seen floating above them before 'whirling into a window'. There were also the overwhelming sounds of shrill voices and discordant shrieks of wicked derisive laughter as this supernatural gathering ensued.

The men turned their backs on the tower and were confronted momentarily by the image of a 'Satanic face with gleaming eyes', and their candles extinguished.[10]

As the men cried out for help, suddenly the tower 'was plunged into darkness' and the coven of witches and their familiars quickly departed. Only the sound of the approaching storm remained to be heard.

In their rush to leave the place, the men became disorientated in the dark-

ALL HALLOWS' EVE

Figure 44: The Gleaming Eyes (© depositphotos)

ness and the raging storm that enveloped them, spending the remainder of the night trapped on the hill until their rescue on the following morning.

Their actions resulted in substantially improved prosperity for the farmer and his family, possibly explained by the following sentiment:

> '…it must have been after midnight when he [the Devil] blew them [the candles] out',[11] and so no longer Hallows' Eve when the spirits joined the living.

****

There can no Hallows' Eve tale without briefly invoking the black cat, and the superstitions that have plagued this poor unfortunate. Depending upon your viewpoint, this witches' familiar is either a lucky charm or an afflic-

HALLOWEEN SPIRITS

tion and portent of bad fortune.

There is no better way to truly observe this unique feline than at the legendary royal 'cat's funeral'.

This strange, sombre and rare ceremony is convened only for mourners who are also cats – black or mostly black cats in particular, as befitting such a solemn occasion. The procession of these four-legged mourners is a queer sight to behold; with all cats wailing and howling together and sounding almost like singing.[12] The small coffin is borne by [eight] cats and is marked with a crown and sceptre as assigned to royalty.[13]

The riddle to this funeral is which of these mysterious felines will next assume the mantle of King of the Cats after the recently departed? Every household cat that learns of the funeral surely believes that it must be them.

'As different as a moonbeam from lightning, or frost from fire.'

Emily Brontë, *Wuthering Heights (1847)*

Figure 45: The Next King (© depositphotos)

THE GRANDE PARADE

'...At Halloween, when fairy sprites
Perform their mystic gambols,
When ilka witch her neebour greets,
On their nocturnal rambles;
When elves at midnight-hour are seen
Near hollow caverns sportin,
Then lads an' lasses aft convene,
In hopes to ken their fortune,
By freets that night...' [1]

Janet Little, *On Halloween, (1792)*

What better way to finish Hallowe'en than with a grand parade of all and sundry. A grandiose procession of the living suitably disguised in costume and ephemeral mysterious spirits from beyond, boldly marching to the wild raucous music of trumpets, saxophones, flutes, guitars, banjos, fiddles and drums.

Gracefully leading the merry throng are the banshees, ghosts and phantasms slipping silently across the ground, with their long shrouds and gossamer veils wafting behind in long sinuous streaks. Next follow the witches astride their flax broomsticks; flying too close to the ground and cackling in hysterical shrieks. Some carry black cats, bats and ravens whilst other creature familiars pursue them closely.

The clattering of a rampant troop of skeletons and the clanking of chains dragged by ghastly pirates drowns out the music of the parade, yet still provide quite a spectacle of such phantoms. These are closely followed by

HALLOWEEN SPIRITS

a swarming rabble of demons, goblins, ghoulish-beings and shadow entities, jostling and pushing each other in turn with small pitchforks and other implements.

Toward the back of the parade are the illuminated grinning jack-o'-lanterns hauled in an olde wooden cart drawn by a phantom stead, and surrounded by a spirited group of pumpkin-headed goblins on foot.

At the rear of the procession are the unworldly musicians, and what a supernatural band they look. '…Mist-like they glide across the heath—a weird and ghostly band…'[2] Their instruments generate shrill piercing sounds like a howling wind interspersed with sweetly harmonious melodic notes, haunted by the incessant rhythmic beat of drums. Whatever the music, it blends perfectly with the array of Hallowe'en characters in this grand parade.

Figure 46: This way to the Grand Parade (© depositphotos)

THE GRANDE PARADE

Figure 47: Come join the Parade (© depositphotos)

Although the grand parade is a time for all to enjoy themselves, it is also a time of personal spontaneity and fervent enthusiasm for the participants. Each plays their role in the celebration.

A ghost may be harmless, well-meaning and fun, or gloomy and intent in frightening all around it with mischievous haunting intent. A banshee should not be upstaged by these open-air spirits, and should provide the mandatory wailing and mournful shrieking essential for a veiled shadow, whilst gliding effortlessly across the ground.

HALLOWEEN SPIRITS

The witches have many incantations to cast and dances to perform, with broom twirled by hand and accompanied by their familiars, or perhaps hopping to a sprightly jig with one of the passing demons. These fearsome horned devils with pointed ears and a tail mostly dance alone in a wild display of flailing arms, kicking legs and shaking of the head, putting on quite a display.

The Grim Reaper and fellow skeletal figures crackle their bones and drag clanking chains in time to the music, sometimes being overrun by the flurry of small bogies, goblins and sprites who scurry throughout the length of the parade. These mischievous characters tumble, roll and sprawl about, causing confusion and mayhem, before leaping and bustling through the throng.

EPILOGUE

Figure 48: Enjoy the Festivity (© depositphotos)

HALLOWEEN SPIRITS

Hallowe'en – the ancient Celtic festival originating at the close of autumn on 31st October and the onset of darkness of the approaching winter. A time of feasting to celebrate the harvest and the prolific abundance of food from the fields, as well as the imbibing of copious alcoholic beverages, presumably extracted and distilled from the harvested fruit. A time for rowdy revelry, boisterous merriment and much participation in great community festivities.

Hallowe'en also shares its mystical origins with the supernatural beliefs and superstitions associated with the symbolic darkness of 'the Otherworld'. 'On that night of the year, the dead might return to the living … to bedevil humans'.[1] A night like no other when the spirits of the deceased and those who have not lived cross over into this world.

> '… this is the one upon which supernatural influences most prevail. The spirits of the dead [airy visitants] wander abroad, together with witches, devils and mischief-making beings on their baneful midnight errands, and in some cases, the spirits of living persons have the temporary power to leave their bodies and join the ghostly crew'.[2,3]

American poet Arthur Peterson aptly sensed the moment in the following excerpt from his 1912 poem *Halloween*:

> '… When they feel the frosty fingers
> Of the autumn closing round them,
> They forsake their earthborn dwellings,
> Which to earth return and die,
>
> "As befits things which are mortal.
> But these spirits, who are deathless,
> Care not for the frosty autumn,
> Nor the winter long and keen;
> But, from field, and wood, and garden,
> When their summer's tasks are finished,
> Gather here for dance and music,
> As of old, on Halloween." [4]

EPILOGUE

The spirit of Hallowe'en and the bountiful harvest of crops so celebrated in this festivity are to be enjoyed by all, for it is truly a time of merriment and revelry for the participants on this ancient customary occasion.

REFERENCES

CHAPTER 1: The Magik of Hallowe'en
1. Guinness World Records, 'Cutting Edge Haunted House, Fort Worth, Texas', October 2009, *Largest Walk-Through Horror House*, https://www.bizjournals.com/austin/prnewswire/press_releases/Texas/2018/10/15/UN38557Accessed 22 October 2018.
2. Morton, 'Celebrations', in *The Halloween Encyclopedia*, 2011, p.49.
3. Bangs, J.K., 'Hallowe'en', in *Harper's Weekly*, Issue 5 November, 1910.
4. Benton, Joel, 'Hallowe'en', in *Harper's Weekly*, Issue 31 October, 1896.
5. Kelley, 'Sources of Hallowe'en', in *The Book of Hallowe'en*, 1st Ed., 1919, p.3.
6. Bryant, *The Death of the Flowers*, 1888.
7. Coxe, 'Halloween', in *Halloween: A romaunt with lays meditative and devotional*, 1869, pp.10-11.

CHAPTER 2: Bonfyres and Lanterns
1. Coxe, op.cit.,'Halloween (Poem)', p.11.
2. Morton, 'Bonfires', in *The Halloween Encyclopedia*, 2011, p.29.
3. Ibid.
4. Merriam-Webster, The History of 'Jack-O'-Lantern': A man with a lantern, a light on a marsh, and a Halloween pumpkin. https://www.merriam-webster.com/words-at-play/the-history-of-jack-o-lantern, Retrieved 25 October 2018.
5. Whittier, 'The Pumpkin', in *Poems*, 1849, p.330.

REFERENCES

CHAPTER 3: Pranking
1. Morton, op.cit., p.190.
2. McNeil, *Hallowe'en: Its origins, rites and ceremonies in the Scottish tradition*, 1970, pp.29-31.
3. Morton, pp.162-63.

CHAPTER 4: Phantasms, Wicce and Dæmons
1. Letts, 'Hallow E'en, 1914', in *The Spires of Oxford: And Other Poems*,1918, p.8.
2. Kelley, op.cit., 'In Brittany and France', pp.115-116.
3. Borrow, 'Lavengro: The Scholar, The Gypsy, The Priest', in *Macmillan's Illustrated Standard Novel*, 1896.
4. Herrick, Robert,'The Hag', in *Works of Robert Herrick*, 1891, pp.27-28.
5. Kelley, op.cit, p.137.

CHAPTER 5: Bogies and Bretheren
1. Briggs, *A Dictionary of Fairies*, 1976, pp.29-33, p.52.
2. Paull, 'Harvest –Rhyme from an old postcard', in *Creating your Vintage Hallowe'en*, 2014, p.102.
3. Morton, op.cit., 'Banshee', p.21.
4. Ibid.
5. Thiselton Dyer, 'The Banshee', in *Ghost World*, 2000, p.279.
6. Seymour & Neligan, 'Banshees And Other Death-Warnings', in *True Irish Ghost Stories*, 1914, p.184.
7. Ibid., 'Death-Warnings', p.190.
8. Schell, 'Dance of the Dead', in *Werner's Readings and Recitations No.31*, p.192.
9. Firefox: Bioluminescent Fungi, inamidst.com, http://inamidst.com/lights/foxfire, Accessed 9 November 2018.

CHAPTER 6: Hallowe'en Familiars
1. Hugo, Victor, 'The Djinns – Poems of Fancy Section II. Fairies:Elves:Sprites', in *The World's Best Poetry*, Vol. VI Fancy:

HALLOWEEN SPIRITS

Sentiment, 1904, ln 49-53.
2. Wikipedia encyclopedia,'Ghost Bat', Updated 17 June 2018, https://en.wikipedia.org/wiki/Ghost_bat, accessed 31 October 2018.
3. Encyclopædia Brittanica, 'Chiroptera', in Volume 6, 11th Ed.,1911, p.239.
4. Chwalkowski, 'Bat the guardian of night', in *Symbols in Arts, Religion and Culture*, 2016, p.523.
5. Hugo, op,cit, 1904. ln 57-63.
6. Volkan, Vamik D.,'The Cat People Revisited', in *Mental Zoo*, 2014, p.267.
7. Ibid.
8. Kelley, op.cit.,'The Celts', p.11.
9. Starbuck & Thomas, 'Solids and Smokes', in *Cat Colors FAQ: Common Colors*, Cat Fanciers Chat, Archived from original 9 October 2011, https://www.webcitation.org/62ISL6nRl?url=http://fanciers.com/other-faqs/colors.html Retrieved 3 November 2018.
10. Morton, Lisa, 'Halloween and Popular Culture', in *trick or treat: a history of halloween*, 2013, p.161.
11. Poe, Edgar Allan, 'The Black Cat', in *Tales of Mystery and Imagination*, 1908, p.519.
12. Poe, Edgar Allan, 'The Raven', in *New York Evening Mirror*, Issue 29 January, 1845.
13. Spence, *The Magic Arts in Celtic Britain*, 1995, p.84.
14. Witchcraft & Wicca, 'Familiars' in *WitchesLore*, 9 October 2010, www.witcheslore.com/magical-creatures-bookofshadows/familiars. Accessed 4 November 2018.
15. Saxby & Clouston, 'The Corbie', in *Birds of Omen in Shetland with Notes on the Folk-Lore on the Raven and the Owl*, 1893, p.7

.

CHAPTER 7: The Hallowe'en Party
1. Schell, 'Halloween Program', in *Werner's Readings and Recitations No.31*, 1903, pp.24-6.
2. Schell, op.cit.,'Broomstick Train; or Return of the Witches', pp.167-170.
3. Ibid., 'Spook March', p.24,

REFERENCES

4. Benton, Joel, op.cit., 'Hallowe'en'.

CHAPTER 8: Costumed Revelry
1. Carlin, *Brain Droppings*, 1997, p.81.
2. Paull, 'Witches', in *Creating your Vintage Hallowe'en*, 2014, p.89.

CHAPTER 9: Hallowe'en Surprises
1. Schell, op.cit., 'Form 3 - Hallowe'en Invitation Forms', p.18.
2. Paull, op.cit., Celebration and Revelry', p.34.

CHAPTER 10: All Hallows' Eve
1. Field, Eugene, 'Seein'Things', in *Poems of Childhood*, 1904, p.191.
2. Willis, Jim, *The Religion Book*, 2003. p.14.
3. Wilde, 'November Eve', in *Ancient Legends, Mystic Charms, and Superstitions of Ireland*, Vol.1, 1887, pp.145-48.
4. Ibid., p.148.
5. Bowker, 'All Hallows' Night', in *Goblin Tales of Lancashire*, 1883, p.190.
6. Ibid.
7. Thiselton Dyer, 'Hallow Eve- Lancashire', in *British Popular Customs: Present and Past*,1876, p.395.
8. Bowker, op,cit., p.193.
9. Ibid., p.194.
10. Ibid., p.195.
11. Ibid., p.197.
12. Briggs, 'Fairy Beasts', in *The Fairies in Tradition and Literature*, 1967, p.72.
13. Burne, 'Two Folk-Tales from Herefordshire: The King of the Cats', in *The Folk-Lore Journal*, Vol. II, 1884, p.23.

CHAPTER 11: The Grande Parade
1. Little, 'On Halloween', in *Poetical works of Janet Little, The Scotch Milkmaid*, 1792, pp.167-8.
2. Mulholland, Rosa, 'Lay of the Irish Famine', in *Werner's Readings and*

HALLOWEEN SPIRITS

Recitations No.31, 1903, p.175.

CHAPTER 12: Epilogue
1. Morton, 'Samhain and the Celts', in *trick or treat: a history of halloween*, 2013, p.14.
2. Walsh, 'Halloween or All Hallow Even', in *Curiosities of Popular Customs and of Rites*, Ceremonies, Observances and Miscellaneous Antiquities, 1898, p.501.
3. Brand, 'Allhallow Even – Halloween', in *Observations on the Popular Antiquities of Great Britain*, Vol.1, 1853, p.380.
4. Peterson, 'Halloween', in The Poems of Arthur Peterson, 1912, p.31.

BIBLIOGRAPHY

Akhtar,Salman and Volkan, Vamik D. (eds.), Mental Zoo: Animals in the Human Mind and Its Pathology, Karnac Books Ltd, London, Great Britain, 2014.

Borrow, George Henry, *Lavengro: The Scholar, The Gypsy, The Priest*, Macmillan and Co., United Kingdom, 1896.

Bowker, James, *Goblin Tales of Lancashire*, Swan Sonnenschein, London, 1883.

Brand, John, *Observations on the Popular Antiquities of Great Britain: chiefly illustrating the origin of our vulgar and provincial customs, ceremonies and superstitions*, Vol.1, Henry G.Bohn, London, 1853.

Briggs, Katherine Mary, *The Fairies in Tradition and Literature*, Routledge & Kegan Paul, London, 1967.

Briggs, Katherine Mary, *A Dictionary of Fairies: Hobgoblins, Brownies, Bogies and Other Supernatural Creatures*, Allen Lane, London, 1976.

Bryant, William Cullen, *An Autumn Pastoral: The Death of the Flowers*, Nims & Knight, Troy, New York, 1888.

Burne, Charlotte S., *The Folk-Lore Journal*, Vol. II, Elliot Stock for The Folk-Lore Society, London, 1884.

Carlin, George, *Brain Droppings*, Hyperion, New York, 1997.

Carman, Bliss, *et al.*, (eds.), *The World's Best Poetry, Vol. VI Fancy: Sentiment*, John D. Morris and Company, Philadelphia, USA, 1904.

Chwalkowski, Farrin, *Symbols in Arts, Religion and Culture: The Soul of*

HALLOWEEN SPIRITS

Nature, Cambridge Scholars Publishing, Newcastle upon Tyne, United Kingdom, 2016.

Coxe, Arthur Cleveland, *Halloween: A romaunt with lays meditative and devotional*, J.B.Lippincott & Co., Philadelphia, USA, 1869.

Field, Eugene, *Poems of Childhood*, Charles Scribner's Sons, New York, 1904.

Herrick, Robert, Hesperides: Or, *The Works Both Humane & Divine of Robert Herrick, Esq.*, John Williams and Francis Eglesfield, London, 1648.

Holmes, Oliver Wendell Sr., The Poetical Works of Oliver Wendell Holmes, Vol.III, Houghton, Mifflin and Company, Boston, USA, 1893.

Keeley, Ruth Edna, T*he Book of Hallowe'en*, Berwick & Smith Co., Norwood Press, Massachusetts, USA, 1919.

Le Braz, Anatole, *The Legend of The Dead in Lower Brittany: Beliefs, Traditions and Uses of Armoric Breton*, Paris, 1893.

Letts, Winifred Mary, *The Spires of Oxford: And Other Poems*, E.P. Button & Company, New York, USA, 1918.

Little, Janet, *Poetical works of Janet Little*, The Scotch Milkmaid, Air, 1792.

McNeill, Florence Marian, *Hallowe'en:Its origins, rites and ceremonies in the Scottish tradition*, Albyn Press, Edinburgh, Scotland, 1970.

Morton, Lisa, *The Halloween Encyclopedia*, 2nd Ed., McFarland & Company, Jefferson, North Carolina, USA, 2011.

Morton, Lisa, *trick or treat: a history of halloween*, Paperback Edition, Reaktion Books, London, 2013.

Paull, Marion, *Creating your Vintage Hallowe'en: The folklore, traditions and some crafty makes*, Cico Books, London and New York, 2014.

Peterson, Arthur, *Collected Poems -The Poems of Arthur Peterson*, George W. Jacobs & Co., Philadelphia, USA, 1912.

Poe, Edgar Allan, *Tales of Mystery and Imagination*, J.M.Dent & Sons,

BIBLIOGRAPHY

London, 1908.

Pollard, Alfred, Works of Robert Herrick, vol. II, Lawrence and Bullen, London, 1891.

Saxby, Jessie Margaret Edmondston and Clouston, William Alexander, *Birds of Omen in Shetland with Notes on the Folk-Lore on the Raven and the Owl*, AMS Press, Indiana, 1893.

Schell, Stanley, *Werner's Readings and Recitations No.31 – Hallowe'en Festivities*, Edgar S. Werner & Company, New York, 1903.

Scott, Walter, *The Monastery: A Romance*, 1st Ed., Longman, Hurst, Rees, Orme and Brown, London, UK, 1820.

Seymour, St. J.D. & Neligan, H.L., True Irish Ghost Stories, First Edition, Hodges, Figgis and Company, Dublin, 1914.

Spence, Lewis, *The Magic Arts in Celtic Britain*, Constable and Company, London, 1995.

Thiselton Dyer, T.F., *British Popular Customs: Present and Past*, George Bell and Sons, London, 1876.

Thiselton Dyer, J.M., *Ghost World*, Senate, Middlesex, United Kingdom, 2000.

Walsh, William S., *Curiosities of Popular Customs and of Rites, Ceremonies, Observances and Miscellaneous Antiquities*, J.B. Lippincott Co., London, 1898.

Whittier, John Greenleaf, *Poems*, Benjamin B. Mussey & Co., Boston, USA, 1849.

Wilde, Francesca Speranza, *Ancient Legends, Mystic Charms, and Superstitions of Ireland*, Vol.1, Ward and Downey., London, 1887.

Willis, Jim, *The Religion Book: Places, Prophets, Saints, and Seers*, Visible Ink Press, Detroit, Michigan, USA, 2003.

ABOUT THE AUTHOR

Figure 49: A Festive Spirit (© depositphotos)

Simon King is an emerging Australian author who has already published seven books:

Crocodiles and Cocktails: A Decade of Adventure at the Kimberley Frontier

Witchcraft, Whispers, Shadows and Strange Sights: A Journey into the Unknown and Unexpected

ABOUT THE AUTHOR

Marbles, Marella Jubes and Milk Bottles: My Golden Years of Australian Childhood

Robot Awakening: The Time of Artificial Life

On The Edge: Extreme Life

Acetylene Dreams: Far Beyond

Extraterrestrial: Alien Life

Each book encompasses different aspects of life's journey, and engages many interesting historical and contemporary perspectives.

His literary work can be reviewed on the website: **www.sdkauthor.com.**

Simon's fascination with Hallowe'en includes celebrating this unique time of year with a costume party or perhaps joining community celebrations in Australia or elsewhere. This book provides some imaginative guidance on how to thoroughly enjoy such festivities.

www.ingramcontent.com/pod-product-compliance
Lightning Source LLC
Chambersburg PA
CBHW050604300426
44112CB00013B/2061